Written by: LaShonda C. Henderson

ISBN-13: **978-1-7321319-2-7**
ISBN-10: **1-7321319-2-9**
Cover Art by Nigel Simon

Published by: Cshantay Publishing
Copyright 2018

For Freedom, For Love

A special thank you to Nigel Simon for
allowing your lens to show a brightly
colorful world!

I started writing about freedom so you understand....

Yes, life has ups and downs, but YOU are the one with the choice! Live, be your best YOU. There are no flaws, it is all just LIFE

I do not know what you need to be free. I can only share what I know and need...maybe it will jog your memories or set you looking for freedom too.....

That thing you want to do? You know, the one you think is minor or unimportant? The one nagging, bring you pains, waiting for its birth? Someone needs it and they are waiting for you!

Freedom means understanding we ARE a collective, while some are on one frequency, others are on another; it is not a good or bad thing, it just is....

Please realize, sometimes you must pick up that nudge...the thing we ALL need, from a place, frequency, or vibration most would panic from. The canal, YOUR canal, is the only one equipped to bring US the fruit, some call it a lesson, found within.

But you cannot do it, if you will not deliver it, the idea into the world.... So, yes, WE are staring; waiting for you to give up the goods, we know you've got it, believe in YOU, for we already do.

I was at a softball game yesterday, between the innings I sat in the shade and saw this tiny caterpillar hanging from a silk thread. It seemed to have fallen out the tree and the thread was all it had left to get back up; I watched it inch its way...little by little back up into the branches... and I thought...

If it were me would I have given up? If it was you would you have given up?

I mean giants (people), obstacles (wind, birds and the silk breaking) did NOT stop its movement. It made it to the branches higher than most people would be willing to climb, that tiny little thing.

All that to say...do not give up. Like that caterpillar, moving towards its butterfly moment; the Universe needs your transformation.

Put in the work...inch along if you must...but move....

In our quiet time....

We discuss life, my dreams, fears, and love.

In our quiet time...

We discuss life, his past, ways and being.

In our quiet time....

We discuss life, evolving, our next moves, aspirations, and connectedness.

In our quiet time...

We kill the past, speak to the now, our thoughts and the future.

Freedom means...making quiet time loudly productive.

I am not the type to force ideas. I just want to know if you heard mine, because I heard yours.

Freedom means remembering ideas are seeds...plant them and go on your way. It is up to the receiver, to make a choice in letting it die or watering it into fruition

When I was little...food was prepared for us as instructed, we cleaned our plate, whether we liked the food served or not. No matter if we had an allergy, no matter if it made our tummies hurt. We did it because we HAD to! Authority said so!!!!

Now I am an adult, I do not have to eat off a plate handed to me. If I do not like what is on the plate I go somewhere else.

Freedom means being hungry for life but NEVER expecting that just any plate will do! Some of us are starving to the point where you will eat ANYTHING...just because it is in front of you...even if you know it is poison....

Be free...

Seek the "good fruit" because it is seeking YOU

Sometimes, before you sort it out in real life, you must sort it out in your head, dreams, and visions. Freedom means, speaking the word and letting the pieces fall...put the puzzle of your greatness together.

You have time!

I have been anxious! It seems life gives hurdle after hurdle before you get to the finish line....

Freedom means, seeing that baby steps are STILL steps. One piece of good news is worth its weight in gold and joy is hearing the voice of the people you love.

Love and let people love you back, it is liberating.

When I was young, I could not wait to feel the Sunshine on my face, because it meant a NEW DAY was here. You see, I had this thing in me that let the day; pile up hurts, offences and "I should have" moments. At the close of the day, I was heavy spiritually and only the Sunrise of a new day could make the weight fall off.

Freedom means, understanding that each breath is like a sunrise. If stress piles up or hurts and offences rear their head, I address it! Then I drop my shoulders...blow out and go on with life!

You cannot be free until you understand, sunlight IS for renewal but so is your mind. Let your thoughts...rise and set; not controlling you but RENEWING you! It is ok to think a new thing; a new way. It helps you to taste the light in EVERY breath you take.

It is wild to me that, you get to write my story and have the audacity to expect me to be still while you scribble!

You want me to be silent about the pain inflicted, and moreover, expect a smile while I am being pencil whipped.

Freedom means I have a pen and I do not have to write the way YOU want me to it write in permeant ink, except it is on my heart and scribble only scar it not really penetrate deep. So, you write, and I will write too.

You gone get this truth, generations will be my witnesses

Check
Check
Check

Freedom means making lists and checking the boxes off as complete; while understanding the most important box to check is not on your list!

If you want to be free, you are going to have to rest!

You DO deserve guilt free rest, it should always be on the list, if not at the top, on it as a minimum!

I was talking to my Big Daddy this morning, even though he is 80+ he STILL parrots things his Mother taught him...

Freedom means...even when we think we are free, the past is STILL relevant....it is our sounding board, our foundation. So, as you meander through this life, remember, YOU TOO will become somebody's point of reference.

Try hard...to be YOU...nothing more.

And know that IS enough!

Just because

I smile Doesn't mean I am not hurting I had to take a breath to put on this brave face,

Just because

I laugh Doesn't mean it failed to penetrate me I had to remember a happy time to block out the wound

Just because I live

Does not mean you did not kill me...

I worry about a lot of things, but one thing I have never had to question, is the breath I just took and I do not have to question if the next one is coming. Freedom means being thankful for the things that come naturally

There is a difference between evil people and workers of iniquity. Workers of iniquity get up every day and think about new ways to hurt you.

-Ricky Smiley

Freedom means realizing that just as good exists, so does the opposite. Now that you know that; look for the good.

Because the opposite is not a work you want a hand in....

It is funny...

When I comb and style my hair it sheds and looks righteous but it grows slowly. However, when I leave it alone, keep it washed and just pull it back it looks a mess but it grows rapidly!

Freedom means, learning to take your hand off a thing, allowing it to look disorderly so it can grow. We do not have to control everything!

Freedom means....

Celebrating the gift of creation.

I instruct my son:

The selection of a wife/partner is the biggest decision of your life! She will be the MOTHER of your lineage...that choice can create heaven or hell for you. Let it not be a hostile decision...a fun time turned into...let us do the right thing. Let it be a strategy to empower your household AND your community.

Affirmation:
I am not perfect, I do the best I can. But my gift...my womb is beyond my birthing canal. It is this HEART...not just for the baby I birth but all who need loving arms for a reason...or just because.....

I was talking to someone I admire and he mentioned that my writing is very romanticized! I acknowledged that he is correct!

You see, I notice the other side, the violence...fear and turmoil that comes with discovering love. But life, society...celebrates that way too much for my liking...

Freedom means celebrating the small instances of light within love, drowned out by trying to survive this walk called life.

If you want to be free, benchmark some small intimate kindness in your life, more than those divisive harsh episodes that leave trauma on your heart.

You have a choice!

Everyone saves and dreams of going to Disneyland. Somehow, they feel like that experience will fulfill an empty spot of lack; because Mickey has magic right?

Freedom feels like, sitting, playing, and squealing with the heroes who make your life safe but thrilling. Except they wear no suits, but they do have nick names and theme songs.

If you want to be free, realize...the most amazing, magical place in the UNIVERSE should be your home. That is where all the magic begins!

Magic words called affirmations,
Magic acts called kindness
Magic affection called love

No smoke, mirrors or costumes needed but the music of life blasts loudly!

 Be free...love those close to you

Freedom means....

When they say look for the light, they
mean YOUR OWN light.

Only you have the switch....

Turn it on

I am not a person who loves a crowd of people. I do not do cult behavior. I am not a free spirit, gypsy or traveler, those labels do not fit me.

Freedom means knowing what I am...and it is not bound by any energy you choose to give it.

Give me a crowd of flowers, a noisy meadow or simply a window view and I will be content. My way does not have to be your way...but both look like freedom!

Be free find your "noise" of choice....

I cannot change anything but myself....

Freedom means, making sure your mind is controlled by the remote control with the good batteries (thoughts). So, no shaking, moving close or forcing the button, needed! You can turn the channel anytime you want!

Be free.... master the fast forward, pause, and power buttons!

It is your MIND control it!

I challenge you

Go a week...one whole week talking to your friends about ideas and not people!

Can you make it????

Freedom means focusing on outcomes not what other people are doing. Think of it as time wasted if it is not growing you or them.

Can you do it?

Some days you will not feel free.

But my Love, it is simply because you allowed the voices of other people to drown out your own.

If you want to be free, you are going to have to learn to put yourself on timeout.

Be free...get quiet...then speak the hell up! Only you know what you need to be happy....

You deserve some happiness

Do not fool yourself....

Just because atrocities are not happening in front of your face, does not mean they are not happening.

Freedom means if one person is not free, no one is...

Because as soon as the oppressed disappear, someone is else becomes fair game to the oppressor....

If you want to be free...stand up for them...like it is happening to YOU...because really...it is...

If you wait 1 year for something it is called patience.

If you wait 2 years it is called focus.

If you wait three or more it is called determination.

Freedom means if you want something, get it now, it exists already and any waiting is time wasted...tomorrow is not promised!

Be free, go fast after your goals...you CAN reach them...

I was working and this lady was throwing me mad shade and negative energy. I did not want her to feel worse, nor give her a chance to escalate that energy towards me....so instead.... I looked at her and said, "Sorry I need to go."

Freedom means, I decide the energy in which I expose myself. I do this without judgment of the person but rather, gauging the energy they radiate. I do not HAVE to be anywhere where someone else's negative vibration drowns out my neutral one.

I manage my own energy...feeling is a choice...a responsibility...some days I can barely keep the tide from rising in me...much less others...self-care is priceless...use it often!

And I imagine after Juneteenth, when freedom was real to them...they let out a sigh and let themselves slowly begin to love again...without fear of the public market....

I have loved many times in my life...but I have only been IN LOVE once.

It made me into the Woman I am. It set me on a path of growth spiritually and financially.

So, I do not have to say it...look at the outcome and KNOW THAT it IS freedom!

The ability to love is freedom...use it well...

Everyone has this thing about keeping likeminded people around them, but that is not the real world. Freedom means keeping the: Crazy ones- Overly Sensitive-Trigger happy- Miserable – Zealous....

People near you too. Now I did not say be bosom buddies, I said near, an observable distance. I dislike labels but the ones listed, are the types you learn so much from! They embody passion!

Be free, learn from ALL people or else you will miss the light within the world. If you cannot see the world properly, if it is too dark, if you dwell in shade too long, you'll miss the chance to unlock your own chains. Because everyone knows, light blinds you at first, when you exit the dark; it is the passionate ones teach you to orient yourself in all conditions!

Watch them, they know the way!

The other day I was sitting in a chair. Now it was super comfortable, except there was one little place on the right side that poked my leg slightly. It wasn't a pain, but a dull feeling of something being there...

I could have moved, but the comfort of the chair persuaded me to stay...the next day a bruise appeared in the spot that felt that "something".

Freedom means, although comfort maybe nice, that ache of longing you feel...will certainly leave a mark if you do not do something about it......

There are sooooo many people in this world that can do EXACTLY what you do.

Freedom is knowing that, and still understanding that YOU and your ideas are unique. No one sees the world like you!

You are perfectly uniquely the same, so let you be YOU. We need it!

And they tell me....

Prove you are free by standing for freedom like I do. I stand...

But I want to scream...remember when you called me an uncivilized animal, my sister a porch monkey and my brother a thug, it was just the other...

Century
Decade
Year
Month
Day

I signed up to fight for my country. I took a pledge to protect its interests; even though tears run down my face, as I stand... I understand what it means to commit my life...yet somehow, you STILL fail to see my humanity. It seems, you want me to act like you, but never "BE" like you.

But as for me...I just want to "LIVE" as freely as you do...following my pursuit of happiness too...LOVing more than I FEAR.

Freedom means...this is not a political post, it is a life plea...

My mother and I used to sit on the porch and talk about worries, joys, and change...sometimes we laughed sometimes she would light another cigarette and we would both stare into the distance drinking in life.

Conversations are a little richer sitting on the porch...

If you want to be free you are going to have to learn to speak like the world is a porch and honesty is the rocking chair that propels you into the future

Freedom means...titles are made by people; but love is made by those who struggle, endure, and make it through life. It is like having a ripe lemon, sour at first, but after that first taste of shock comes sweetness! But you will not notice unless you keep tasting it, yet every phase is LOVE

Be free...there will be some sour moments, but trust... the good part is coming...the trick is... you must be looking for it, or you will miss it!

Freedom means evolving, understanding that what used to move me, no longer does.

Be free...put down some things to pick up some others...

Freedom means...

Letting go...

If you want to be free, release your grip on life. Feel the air racing by, the atmosphere gripping you and life shifting as you fall into the natural flow of things. Be free...trust the fall....

I know you are tired of people telling you what to do. I know you are sick of all the proposed solutions. So, I will not tell you what to do.

I will just sit here staring into the sky with no purpose, watching the birds soar and the leaves blow in the wind.

You can join me. Or not.

That's Freedom...discovering, that you CAN check out and do nothing.....

I think, most people are afraid of abandonment. I mean, we cling to people, ideas and things that provide comfort...even if it eats us alive mentally and physically, we cling tightly. But the truth is...it boils down to thinking the item, thing or person is the totem for LOVE. So, are we afraid of abandonment, or are we afraid their leaving signifies our worthiness to be loved?

Freedom means...things change...people exit this plane...new life enters this plane...some life transitions...but LOVE does remain. So, stop clinging so tight...you do not lose anything...we recycle experiences...Love does not abandon us it just transforms...

I was telling my son how I learned to appreciate Opera and Classical music. Would you believe it was Bugs Bunny? He taught me how to have tea like a lady, how to move when you need to, how to turn up on people who try to play you and most importantly the power of a hot bath versus becoming dinner.

Freedom means, lessons are EVERYWHERE. Give thanks and receive them generously. The trick is.... understanding it all has relevance...leave/stay, flowers, sunlight, cartoons, and real life...but how will you use it?

When my son was young I taught him to express himself. Then I would test him by saying outrageous things that could not be true and ask him if he agreed with me.

You see, freedom means helping your child to see the world from THEIR vision, then helping them to understand that even YOU can be wrong sometimes. They should trust themselves.

Balance is helping them go beyond the boundaries and blockades they put up against things that are not dangerous... but must be experienced.

What I wrote yesterday, last week, last month, last year, is a reminder of where I was in THAT moment...

I see the progression... the change!

Freedom means.... laying a foundation that you can ALWAYS go back to when needed.

Be free... lay bricks in your life...for YOU are the :

Cornerstone...

Master mason...

Architect for YOUR life...

Everything that happens is the blueprint for you to create a grand structure called, "YOU", so build!

I think the scariest thing about praying is that, the thing I pray for might come true.

Freedom means knowing that people are in positions of power for resources. But the Universe/Most High is the source of the resource! I do not need to pray for things I can see or define...it exits...and if it exists it is AVAILABLE to me...through work!

Let me save my requests for connection and conversation. Because talking to the source is the MOST important part of falling in LOVE....not the things I receive.

Prayer/Meditation/Vibing is intended for your soul...use it well....

Life ain't fair, there is not one freeing thing about hearing that. So now what? Freedom means I do not know, but I am not going to just sit down doing nothing. I will freely give what belongs to ME this heart.

My Momma used to say for every person who thinks they are "bad" there is someone who "badder".

Freedom means knowing when to pop off and when to sit the hell down. Yes your mouth can be a weapon...but even weapons backfire and jam you up. Tread lightly and know exactly what you are asking for....

I do not want to be famous. I want to be a witness to the world changing. Not into one where everyone is rich, or one where I get to be rich alone.

You see...freedom means, understanding that some DO work harder than others. But some love harder too. One is rewarded in money and the other is rewarded in spirit. But which one is REALLY rich?

I want to be comfortable, but the comfort "I" seek ...is being able to lay my head down at night not worried about people who are alone, hurt or broken spirited.

I cannot fix ANYTHING, but I have this LOVE....I'm going to spread it and maybe someone will spread their type of love back to me too....

Balance the riches and the world WILL be free

Freedom means seeing the end goal and remembering.... hard work is required before you reach an extended period of relaxing!

You have this....it feels hard so you can appreciate the softness later!

Feet to the ground, mind to the sky and hands into the dirt.

Freedom means....one foot in front of the other, a step at a time in the right direction. Be whatever you want, but you MUST be willing to.... stand, think, and get dirty! You know what that means.....

If You're feeling sad....

I am that girl who is going to leave you a love note. Not a "get with you note". But a magical arrangement of YOU MATTER note. Because I know what it feels like to think I didn't matter. If I can stop that feeling for YOU...I will.

No reciprocation required.

If you know me, you know I love getting flowers. I love looking at them, planting them, and just touching them in general; they are like tiny blossoms of hope, they survive in some hostile places and turn the environment beautiful.

So, this morning I got up and tossed rose petals from my love gift into my backyard...

Freedom means decorating the world, surroundings, and our spirit with beauty and hope; no one else can do that for us... you deserve some romance...and the greatest there is...I call it living

Life is like a hurricane.... the winds are coming and they will take down the things not set firmly...

Superficial love, will get blown away

"Halfway", "Sort of" and "Kind of" effort will get blown away... Lean the wrong way, watch you will be blown down too! Brace yourself...

Work with the wind, not against it...

No fly away notions
No unfinished projects
No swaying to what "they" want you to do

Stand...lean...make your plans solid...

Freedom means, hearing the alarm...preparing...AND then watching the hurricane breeze over...waiting calmly for the minimal cleanup, because no plan is perfect...but preparation makes it easier...

You CAN do this...

While there are a billion of people in the world to share in your being happy. A billion literally.

But it is amazing, that a person singles out 1 and says I want to be happy with them. This may be wrong thinking. Maybe we are supposed to be happy with many...in many different ways...

But, there may be that 1 person that makes you happier than most. Cherish them...they chose you over a billion other people...so enjoy the moment.... seeking no ownership....

Freedom means knowing YOU make you happy and other people supplement that happiness.

Every party I hug the wall. I sit off to the side and grin like a kid at all the fun everyone is having. That is fun to me...smiling...giggling and feeling comfortable.

Freedom means knowing I can do the usual or talk to people I don't know.

It makes me grow too big for this "shell"...heck it may break it off my being and I'm ok with THAT!

The very first thing to touch your lips in the morning should be praise and water. If you can do that unrestricted... You ARE FREE...

Nothing on this earth makes you better than another person. Things do not define you, spirit does. Keep it light, forgiving, and ready to bond.

We ARE interlocked.

But....if you want to be free you are going to HAVE to dig for the most precious treasure ever.... YOUR LOVE

I think I spent too much time trying to make other people feel comfortable...by talking like them, joking like them and being mean like them. I want to spend more time loving, like ME. Freedom feels like ME, BEING ME

Yesterday....

I hopped on a bike. Not a stationary bike, but a two-wheel youthful steel frame of freedom. As I peddled, I am sure I was smiling like a lunatic...hair blowing, wind whipping my exposed skin and my body screaming with excitement / memory of my childhood.

You see, I rode it in the street, the forbidden street. Something inside of me lit up with liberation. Only to be disrupted by the sound of my Son yelling, "Mom get out the street, you don't have on a helmet." Then I realized that as free as I felt in that moment...I too am an oppressor...

Life is a full circle...you can be free ANY time you want to.....but as you taste freedom...teach the way just as hard as you teach oppression. Rules are nice...but knowing when to break them is nicer....

Be free...flow...then teach the way...

I never prayed for a man to be with me
I never prayed for money
I never prayed for my circumstances to change

I prayed for STRENGTH

You see, if you want to be free, you are going to have to endure the lesson, lest you repeat it again. Face it, own what happens, decide where you want your future to go.... then act.

I am not saying you will get it right on the first try.

I am saying, until you can OWN your circumstances, you cannot have the power to do anything about them.

Bulk up...love is life's protein...you have this! Love says so

When it is all said and done.... peace is what we are all seeking.... Freedom feels a lot like, laying in loving arms or laying comfortably against a body of love...staring at the chaos of the world while our souls watch each other.

One thing I always pray is...

Please let me be just as understanding of people as I want them to be of me. Help me to remember, as I make mistakes and want them forgiven, others seek that same grace. As I grow into being me, I will shatter some images of who people thought I was and that is ok.

My choices belong to me. Opinions belong to the person that utters them.

But my outcomes will be shared by all who are in communion with me. May I remember love in each choice.

And that my friends...is FREEDOM!

I intend, I speak, I act, I honor the outcomes

Look around.

No really look around.

Think back 10 years ago.

Think back 5 years, 5 mins.

Freedom feels like, being thankful.

Your right NOW is light years away from your "back then".

So much happens daily...If we blink we miss the good parts... Freedom means love for your now...with or without the blessings you asked for... Be present

Please remember the movies, shows and music...plays a role in kids' psychological well being.

Speak and they listen....no matter who it is talking!

Freedom means.... teaching that things have value, but they are NOT your sole value! Words are treasures, they are building blocks!

WORDS create a world....so, what would you have their or your world be?

If you only watch TV...you will see the world through your "TV" experience. If you only party, you will see the world through that life. If you only go to church, yep you guessed it, the world will be a church experience.

Freedom means balance. Experience the world from multiple angles, so you can decide what soothes your spirit. Because if you are not careful, your "normal" will become a prison. Be free, look around and you might find paradise is here on earth.

Today is another day to touch the heavens while standing on EARTH. So, let me send my prayers to the Ether... But let me act here in THIS place... While being thankful for the ability to LOVE my NOW.

I am not better than my brothers
I am not better than my sisters
I am a product of my ancestors
Everything in ME is in THEM
WE are all cogs in the wheel of life
Hoping we turn towards the light
My gift is NOT more important than
YOUR gift

Freedom means understanding that
without every piece of the puzzle
working together, there is no finished
picture....

"I AM because WE are"

Use your gift so we ALL grow

Listen it takes 6 weeks for the military to break you. How many weeks have you spent breaking YOU down? Freedom means choosing who you become!

I am my own person. Exclusive of others but inclusive because I exist!

Freedom means knowing who I am, what I like and what is needed for my growth.

Vulnerability should not be an attack word, but rather an acknowledgement of imperfection!

Be free, without labels...unbound by propaganda exclusive of judgement without understanding!

I will never be perfect, but I do try my best. My best is all I have to offer and it is more than enough.

And THAT is freedom

Nothing shocks me anymore. I have seen some pretty bad things and some amazing things too!

Freedom means...preparing for what needs to happen. Letting some things go and embracing some new things/ideas. Simply because you want to... because you need to expand outside of your box....

Be free...but don' t be NOBODY's fool!

Your time, heart and mind are valuable! Do what you want because you want to...no holds barred...while placing no blame!

Freedom begins, the moment you decide to do something about your bondage.... Go within, cut some ropes, knock over some dated ideas and make room for new concepts!

People ask why do I see the world through such rose colored lenses. Here is a prayer we used to repeat as kids...

"Thank you for the world so sweet, thank you for the food we eat...thank you for EVERYTHING...Amen"

No matter what ills were going on in me or out in the world I used to think..."Well it MUST be sweet somewhere and I am thankful for that place and I hope someday I will go there.

I did find that place as an adult...it is "IN ME". I go there often and I am thankful!

This man who wanted to date me lavished me with praise. He told me how beautiful, how smart, and witty I was...until he realized I would not date him. Then he called me a stuck-up b#@ch.

Freedom is not having to lay down on my back because you complimented me. I am the same woman with a yes or no.

Let me live.

"HANDS"

AND I stood there
Hand out stretched
Asking them to see my humanity
But they would not reach back

AND I stood there
Begging to be seen
Asking them to acknowledge me
But they would not look my way

AND I stood there
Offering all of my life
Asking them to share in the blessing
They turned to me

Taking everything, but never seeing ME
Picking me apart
Asking me to give more
But I had nothing left

But this outstretched hand
Offering love
Asking them to share theirs too
But they did not

And I stood there
Hand outstretched
Asking for nothing
But waiting for life
For balance

I put my hand down
And placed it on my
Life
My heart
Asking for me

And I am still waiting for an answer

Freedom means, standing in the shoes of another person's experience, with no judgement, yet seeking understanding. I will sing the lyrics, repeat the stories and drink in the fables...That is love for the culture.

I am just a woman on this journey towards ME, like you are for YOU. We all get there differently....so experience someone else's view.... not as comparison...but as confirmation that individual life in your community is diverse.

Look at the shapes of leaves on ONE tree...they have a general shape, but if you look really close none of them are EXACTLY the same.... yet we STILL call that tree by its scientific name. We are THAT....differently the same....

And that is OK! More than that...it is NORMAL!

So BE....we need your "YOU-ness"

We go to school for 12-13 years to get a diploma. The lessons found within those walls teach assimilation into American society. Most DO NOT understand a world view until they reach college.... there you learn that everything you have been taught.... was a taste of someone's truth but not the ONLY or REAL truth?

No, College does not determine your mental ability. But it does allow you room to decide what interests you most, and the foundational knowledge needed to make it a profession!

Freedom means...choosing to go to college or not. But the key thing you miss by not going is learning a new way to see the world. Yes, some do this organically...but some need guiding. Do not knock them for trying. Do not look at college as the same style of learning from high school...they are two different animals!

College is for EVERYONE...but only a few decide that is the direction for them to CHOOSE and that is ok too!

I have read hundreds of books in my lifetime. Some by world renown Doctors, Spiritual Leaders, Historians, Scientists, Master Storytellers and Social Psychologists. But....Not one of them can tell me what it means to be ME.

So, if they cannot describe me, and they do not have a nice neat category for me...the so-called experts I mean...why would I concern myself with your definition of ME?

Freedom means...I have my own label for ME and there is no room on my chest to wear any haphazard one you drew up in the back of your mind with limited facts. So, keep it....

My label was carefully drawn, I even added some beautiful designs for presentation... but it is clear enough for you to see my NAME. And unless you address me by THAT I cannot hear YOU! I determine ME... just like you get to determine YOU!

Change....

This world is rapidly changing. Freedom means either you go with the flow...the stream of the current that exists or create your own path.

Be free trailblaze your path...but document your change just in case you go the wrong way...that way you can go in another direction if need be!

Never wait for someone else to make you feel worthy. Freedom means, alone...in a group or in a crowd....

You matter!

There is no competition in this world. There is only an "I want that" issue.

Every goal, every game, every mechanism we use to "win" is a symptom. We want to feel like we matter!

If I conquer that THING, the moment I am rewarded...I MUST be important... right? But...the same people who appear to cheer, may be the same ones whispering about how you didn't "EARN" IT righteously!

You'll never do it their way...because you can't please those who have an "I want that" mentality too. They are looking for your misstep, so they can claim what you seek. They want it too!

That is not competition...that is a heart problem.

Freedom means...I want to conquer, to increase my own body of wealth...my knowledge...and I want to deposit into your body of wealth as well. I conquer to show those with me how to do it and I learn when I am with those who conquer too.

There is no competition...we all win

As a parent, the most damaging thing you can do is promote unhealthy competition against your kids. It makes them distrust one another, and if you cannot trust your sibling, well who can you trust.

Freedom means untangling and identifying the seeds of discord and plucking them from your garden of growth like weeds.

Promote cooperation and building as a family unit. Stroke their egos for what they are good at as individuals not as a one up on the next child.

When I was young I met this woman. She had a man she lovvvvveeeed! I mean worshiped the ground he walked on.

He did not treat her right, he cheated and talked foul to her in her face AND in the streets. She clung faithfully for yearssss! I did not judge I just supported her, let her lay her head and heart on my shoulder when she grew tired. She finally left him and was devastated! But guess what? A year later she was married...to man who loved her like she loved...happier than I had ever seen her in LIFE!

Freedom means, loving full force...knowing when to let go...and knowing when what you are looking for is in front of your face!

If you want to be free, know your heart WILL get bruised! But also know, it can be repaired! Do not give up...right now may not be what you want...but your story is NOT over!

Be free... give yourself a CHANCE! No waiting...take the leap!

Four years ago, I had a piece of paper on my wall with four topics. If you are friends with me, I mean deep friends... you heard me talking about it. I finished that list last year....

Now I am working on a new journey. I have yet to write the vision...but it is coming....

Freedom means....

Setting your OWN standard and then setting a new one. Because you can be what you dream...with effort! Speak...write...do

Have patience Freedom means, after the rain...the good of the Earth appears... flowers, grass, and fruit. All things of beauty and substance. Be still, enjoy the downpour...

And if you know how "they" will act, the next question is how will "you" act.

Freedom means making no excuses for the way others move, it is accountability for the way you move. Say, "I will do what I can with what "I" know."

The only prison that can really do damage to you....is one you build.... everything else is background noise

Be objective not subjective....no bowing

When I'm writing...
I hold my breath.
Not on purpose though
I don't even know I'm doing it
Until the words come out
They tumble
S L O W L Y
void of air
Until it all is out
And then I exhale
That relief feels it has been
Where ever those words came from
They both feel like they entered
From Life
But I'd call it
Love

Yes, Love IS real

Yesterday. I met the kindest woman. She was celebrating Love day by herself, due to her husband being in Afghanistan. It put life into perspective. Even though she was missing him fiercely she directed the energy into making the people around her feel loved.

I admire that.

Freedom means not being bound to just your own needs. It means meeting those of others too.

There are so many paths to the same place.

Some longer
Some shorter
Some with high elevation
Some with a scenic view
Some zig zag
Some are a direct route

Freedom means....

Knowing you can drive whatever road you want, for whatever reason. But what you cannot do... is drive a road for someone else. They determine their route and they do not have to tell you why! Even if they ride with you...they will see the world from a passenger perspective...not a driver!!!! Be free, but most importantly....

You just focus on staying on YOUR road!

When I was young 15, 20, 30 a year ago, last week...

If my man did something I did not like, I would up the anty, bring out the microphone and start the circus. It made me feel powerful over my feelings and seeing shock in his face made me feel arrogant and above him. I mean, how can my energy be valuable, yet I intentionally use it to hurt him? Because really, I would sink lower than he was...

Freedom means if I hurt the ones I love, it is like hurting me. LISTEN CAREFULLY. If I hurt from a place of hurt.... hurt spreads like wildfire and for those moments...it feels like love never existed.

If you want to be free.... leave the arena. The food is lame, the crowd is fickle and it is hard to find the bathroom (aka a place of relief), much less an exit when you are ready to go....

Many times, in my life non-minority people were my biggest supporters. Not because I was trying to be like ANYONE...but because the vision I was seeking was FAMILIAR.

I heard in my community a lot of whys, nos and you think that will work...because people who feel oppressed do not know how to help you out of oppression...yet....
EVERY single person is responsible for stroking the dreams of each other...skin color not being a factor. Reality means understanding THAT it is NOT case in the real world. People seek those who look like them and have the same financial and social values.

Freedom means...if I find a way to lift the foot of oppression off my neck...I reach back to help the hurting stand like I stand with some relief.....but understanding it may not be a choice they are used to seeing...and they get to decline my outreach. That is not arrogance, Uncle Toming nor selling out.

It is LOVE....the best I can offer...choose

I tell people all the time, do not pick up what does not belong to you!

Yet...it is hard.

Freedom sometimes means...loving people you just met enough to carry a burden with them. I am not saying own the burden, just poke a hole in the balloon (if they let you) to release some pressure. Community exists to shoulder a shared mission...Advise me, care for me and let me do the same in return....

But do NOT forget, people have a choice to share the burden or not....

Be free....

love....

then give back what is not yours!

Growth is my focus....

If you are happy, good. If you are not, change. It is that simple. I do what I love, I am a part of something bigger than me, but that is not what makes me feel important or free or good about me...

Work is a calling to use your gifts...a chance to fine tune them...to be liberal in determining your direction....

Yes, I WILL start my own business, not carry someone else's logo, and call it mine...but a start up from the ground...but right NOW...

I'm content...I'm learning...I'm being fine tuned

Freedom means looking around and DECIDING what works for your NOW, while preparing for your NEXT in the background....

What is your job teaching you?

When they said Zombies were coming years ago, we all laughed at the people preparing their selves. It is not funny anymore. They were right...the Zombie apocalypse is here...look around.... protect your spirit!

The run of events shout:

Don't read, we'll tell you what you need to know in our news cycle.

Don't speak, wait we do not need your opinion, we'll tell you what to say.

Don't run, fear is in your head, never mind the fact that those who comply end up dead too.

Don't ask for freedom, we'll give you what you need to be happy.

If you want to be free, call this thing what it is...a cage designed to keep you on the wheel turning viciously, but going nowhere.

Freedom means looking for the latch, opening the cage and moving towards the source of light and healing...mentally and physically....

I tell you about me, so you will think about YOU.

That is what freedom is...thinking. I could tell you what to do, but that would make me your Dictator not your Ally....

In this journey called life, you make your own path...people can go with you but not walk it for you...

Think deep thoughts and shallow ones too...then BE....

You can Find
LaShonda on Facebook at

www.facebook.com/loveandotherthoughts

on
Instagram at
LoveAuthorLCH

on
the Web at
www.Cshantaypublishing.weebly.com

www.Cshantaypublishing.org

www.ingramcontent.com/pod-product-compliance
Lightning Source LLC
Chambersburg PA
CBHW021205020426
42331CB00003B/214